GET SPORTY

Cricket

Edward Way

WAYLAND

First published in 2015 by Wayland

Copyright © Wayland 2015

All rights reserved.
Dewey Number: 796.3'58-dc22
ISBN: 978 0 7502 9488 1
Library ebook ISBN: 978 7502 7647 4

10 9 8 7 6 5 4 3 2 1

MIX
Paper from
responsible sources
FSC® C104740
FSC
www.fsc.org

Editor: Nicola Edwards
Designer: www.rawshock.co.uk

Wayland

An imprint of

Hachette Children's Group

Part of Hodder & Stoughton

Carmelite House

50 Victoria Embankment

London EC4Y 0DZ

Picture acknowledgements

All photographs by Clive Gifford
except for (to come). The author and
publisher would like to thank (to come)
for their help with the photographs for
this book.

Printed in China.

An Hachette UK Company
www.hachette.co.uk
www.hachettechildrens.co.uk

CONTENTS

Play cricket!   4

Get started   6

Kwik cricket   8

Know the rules   10

Hit it!   12

Different strokes   14

Build an innings   16

Bowl it!   18

Take a wicket   20

Fielding   22

Catch it!   24

Keeping wicket   26

Making the team   28

Glossary   30

Resources   31

Index   32

PLAY CRICKET!

Cricket is a great team sport for boys or girls. The full game is played by two teams, each with 11 players. Players in the fielding team bowl the ball and try to stop runs being scored by the batting team.

GAME PLAY

Pairs of players bat and try to score runs. When a player is out (see page 11) he or she is replaced by another member of the team. This continues until ten players are out or until an agreed number of balls has been bowled. Then, the other team takes its turn to bat, known as an innings.

BOWLING

1 A bowler runs up to the wicket and bowls the ball overarm. In a full game of cricket she will bowl six balls in a row, which is called an over.

2 The bowler tries to bowl accurately to get the batsman out or to make it hard for the batsman to score runs.

BATTING

1 The batsman stands at the other end of the pitch waiting for the ball. As it arrives, he has to decide what sort of shot to play.

2 The batsman brings his bat back and steps into the shot. The fielder behind the stumps is called the wicketkeeper. He is ready in case the ball comes to him.

3 The batsman hits the ball into a gap, away from players in the fielding team.

4 The batsman and his batting partner decide to take a run. They run to the opposite ends of the pitch, crossing in the middle.

5 To complete a run, the bat must touch the ground close to the stumps. Batsmen can take more than one run if they want to…

6 …But they must be careful. If a fielder hits the stumps with the ball before they ground their bat, they will be out, run out.

GET STARTED

Cricket is played on a large field. Fielders stand in different places around the field to stop runs and to take catches.

THE PITCH AND WICKET

A cricket field is split into two sides. The side behind a (right-handed) batsman is called the leg side. The other side is called the off side. This diagram shows some of the many fielding positions.

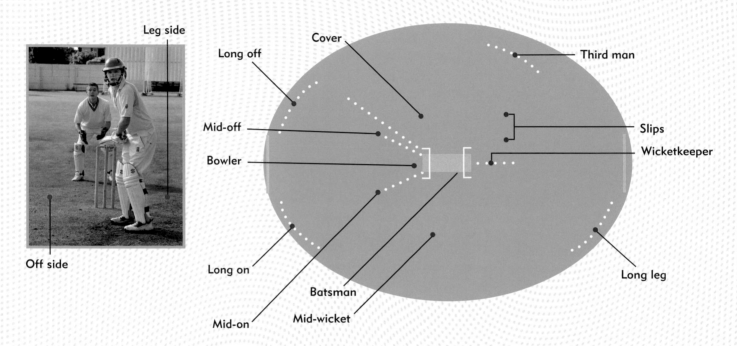

Leg side

Off side

Long off

Cover

Third man

Mid-off

Slips

Bowler

Wicketkeeper

Long on

Long leg

Mid-on

Batsman

Mid-wicket

In the middle of the field is a narrow strip called the pitch. At each end is a wicket made up of stumps and bails (see page 7). The lines around the stumps are called creases.

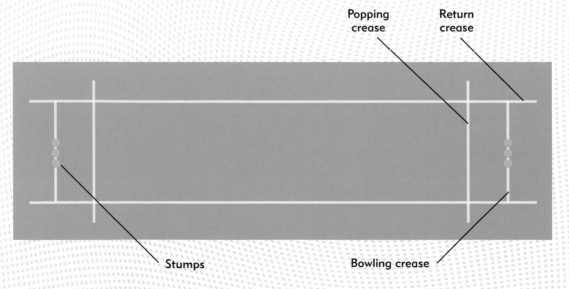

Popping crease

Return crease

Stumps

Bowling crease

A wicket is made up of three vertical stumps and two wooden bails that rest on top. To be out stumped, run out or bowled (see page 11), one or both of the bails have to come off the stumps.

BAT AND BALL

A cricket ball is hard and shiny and comes in different sizes. Younger players may play with a size 4 ball.

A cricket bat is made of wood with a wide blade and a round handle. The handle is covered in a rubber sleeve called the grip.

CLOTHING AND KIT

A batsman, bowler and wicketkeeper all wear white cricket trousers and shirts. The wicketkeeper may wear a sleeveless cricket jumper to keep warm. Players wear trainers with good grip for the ground or special cricket boots.

Leg pads protect shins and knees from being rapped by a hard cricket ball. An arm guard is a pad that protects the lower arm and elbow. Players sometimes also wear a chest pad under their shirt.

Batting gloves are heavily padded to protect the fingers. If you are playing with a proper cricket ball you must wear a helmet. This should fit comfortably and has a grille at the front to stop the ball hitting your face.

KWIK CRICKET

Kwik cricket is a fun, safe way for boys and girls aged 5-11 to start playing cricket. Everyone has a turn at batting and bowling. An over lasts four balls and all the overs are bowled from the same end of the pitch.

PLAYING THE GAME

There are usually eight players a side in a Kwik cricket team. Teams are mixed with both boys and girls who can all wear shorts or tracksuit bottoms.

Kwik cricket is played with brightly-coloured plastic bats, balls and stumps. There is no need for pads or helmets. The ball is light and it won't hurt if it hits you.

In a full sized game of cricket, the pitch is 22 yards (20.1 metres) long. In Kwik cricket, it is 16 yards (14.6 metres) long.

1 A Kwik cricket innings lasts for eight overs. A bowler bowls overarm. If you cannot yet bowl overarm, you are allowed to bowl underarm.

2 The batting team is divided into four pairs with each pair batting for two overs each.

3 After each over, the fielders all change positions. This gives everyone a turn to bowl and a chance to be the wicketkeeper.

SCORING

A team starts with 200 runs. Players can add to their team's score just like in regular cricket, by hitting the ball and taking a run...

...But if they are out, such as here by being bowled, their team loses five runs. The pair bats for two complete overs, no matter how many times each player is out.

Pairs of batsmen bat until eight overs are completed, then the other team bats. The team with the most runs wins!

KNOW THE RULES

A full game of cricket is run by two umpires. They stand on the field during a match and make sure players follow all the rules (called laws) of cricket.

LEARNING THE LAWS

Cricket's laws are complicated but you can ask your teacher or coach to help you learn about them. Some rules are to do with bowling the ball fairly.

1 This ball has been sent wide of the batsman. The umpire will signal a wide by sticking his arms straight out. In most forms of cricket, one run is added to the score and the ball is bowled again.

2 A bowler's front foot must not be over the batting crease as he bowls. If this happens he umpire will signal a no ball. The ball will be bowled again and one run will be added to the score.

SCORING

The edge of a cricket field is called the boundary. It is marked out by a rope or cones. If the ball is hit, bounces on the ground and then rolls onto or over the boundary, the batsman scores four runs.

If the batsman hits a big shot that sends the ball over the boundary before it lands, six runs are added to the batsman's score.

OUT!

There are several ways in which a batsman can be out apart from being run out (see page 5). Here are some of the most common ways.

1 Caught – the batsman's bat or glove holding the bat hits the ball and a fielder catches it before the ball hits the ground.

2 Bowled – the bowler bowls the ball and it hits the stumps, knocking the bails off.

3 LBW (Leg Before Wicket) – the ball heads towards the stumps but hits the batsman's pads first. There are no LBWs in Kwik cricket.

4 Handled Ball – batsmen must not use their hand to stop the ball hitting the stumps.

HOWZAT!

If a bowler and his team-mates think they have got a batsman out, they must appeal to the umpire by shouting, 'how's that? (which sounds like 'howzat!'). The umpire then decides if the batsman is out or not. When an appeal is successful, the umpire shows that a batsman is out by raising a single index finger.

HIT IT!

You need good skill and judgement to bat well in cricket. It takes lots of practice to be able to judge each ball as it comes towards you and to choose the best shot to play.

BE READY

A batsman needs a good batting grip and stance to feel comfortable, balanced and ready to move in any direction. Batsmen stand on the edge of their batting crease. Sometimes when the ball bounces sharply, they step back to play a shot. At other times they may need to step forward to hit a different type of shot.

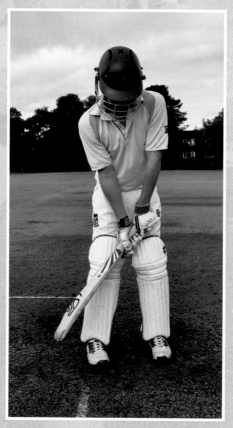

When you grip a cricket bat your top hand should be quite firm and your bottom hand a little more relaxed. The back of your top hand should face the direction of the ball.

This batsman has a good stance with his feet shoulder-width apart. His knees are slightly bent but he stands as tall as possible.

The bat rests lightly on the ground just behind his back foot.

THE FORWARD DEFENSIVE

The forward defensive is a common shot played to a good length ball (see page 16) that is heading towards your stumps.

1 As the bowler comes in to bowl, the batsman turns his head so that his head and shoulders point down the pitch. He swings his bat back straight before playing a shot.

2 The batsman starts his shot by swinging the bat backwards as the ball is bowled. This is called the backlift. The batsman keeps his eye on the ball as it comes towards him.

3 He moves his front foot forward close to where he thinks the ball is going to bounce. He gets his body's weight over his front foot.

4 He brings the bat down smoothly and as straight as he can. He shows as much of the flat front face of bat to the ball as possible.

5 He keeps his front elbow high and his bottom hand on the bat relaxed to kill the ball's speed as it drops down in front of him.

A backwards defensive is a similar shot to the forward defensive. You play it as you step back into your crease.

DIFFERENT STROKES

Choosing the right shot to play will allow you to hit the ball into gaps between fielders to score runs. It also helps you to defend against different types of bowling. The more strokes you learn and master, the more chance you'll have of staying in and scoring runs.

TOP TIP Build up your confidence by practising batting strokes with your coach and in cricket nets.

PUSHES AND FORCES

You can turn backwards and forwards defensive strokes (see pages 12-13) into shots that can score you runs.

1 This batsman angles the bat slightly to play a push shot out on the leg side. The shot is like a forward defensive but the batsman pushes through the ball a little more firmly.

2 The ball travels safely away from fielders. The batsman calls to his partner to make a run and sprints hard to the other end.

3 A backwards forcing shot is similar to a backwards defensive. The batsman swings the bat down a little faster to hit the ball harder to try to score runs.

4 The bat punches through the ball, sending it racing back along the ground. Make sure your body is over the ball and you hit the ball down. Otherwise you might give the bowler a chance to catch you out.

THE LEG GLANCE

You can play a leg glance shot to a ball which is travelling wide of leg stump.

1 The batsman turns his body so that his chest faces the front. He gets his head over the ball and his weight over his front foot.

2 The batsman brings the bat forward straight ahead of him. He flicks his wrists to angle the bat as it hits the ball.

3 He tries not to hit the ball too hard. He needs to time his shot well to make the ball travel away to the leg side.

THE COVER DRIVE

Drives are some of the most attractive and important shots you can learn. You play them with your bat coming down as straight as possible.

1 The batsman spots that the ball is coming wide of his off stump. He starts to step forward.

2 He moves his front foot to get close to where the ball will land. He points his shoulders at the landing spot and shifts his weight over his front foot.

3 The batsman swings the bat down straight so that the whole of the face of the bat connects with the ball.

4 The bat follows through so that the batsman's back shoulder travels under his chin. The ball goes racing away safely along the ground on the off side.

As a batsman you have to mix attack and defence to avoid getting out and to score runs. Keep your eyes on the ball and decide quickly where you think it will land and which shot you will play.

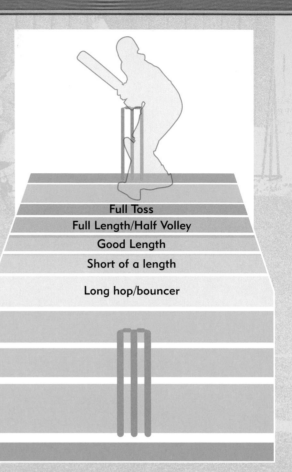

Full Toss
Full Length/Half Volley
Good Length
Short of a length
Long hop/bouncer

LINE AND LENGTH

The line of the ball is where across the pitch the ball comes towards you. The length of a ball is how far up the pitch it makes its first bounce. A short-pitched ball bounces in the middle of the pitch and rises high. You need to use a variety of shots to play balls of differing line and length.

The diagram on the right shows the different bowling lengths a batsman can face.

PRO PLAY

The sweep is an attacking shot which sends a ball away on the leg side. Here, England batsman Jonathan Trott swings his bat in a wide path. His bat face almost faces the ground as he hits the ball. This keeps the ball low.

1 When you first come out to bat, you can ask the umpire to tell you when your bat is in front of the middle stump. This is called taking guard. You are allowed to scratch a mark on the pitch as a reminder.

2 This batsman faces a short high ball. He decides not to play it and pulls his bat out of the way.

3 When the ball threatens his stumps he needs to play defensively. Here, he plays a forward defensive shot, watching the ball carefully.

4 When a ball is short and wide, the batsman can play an attacking shot. This shot is called a cut. It sends the ball racing away to the boundary for four runs.

TOP TIP When you are batting, make your calls for a run to your partner loud and clear. If you don't think a run is on, shout "No!" loudly and quickly.

BOWL IT!

Bowling takes lots of practice and help from a teacher or coach. You need to grip the ball correctly, take a good run-up and then release the ball powerfully, while aiming it accurately.

SEAM BOWLING

There are different types of bowling. Most young cricketers start with seam bowling. This is where you try to land the ball on the pitch on its stitched seam, hoping it will move sideways a little off the seam to trick the batsman.

THE GRIP

Place your middle and first finger either side of the ball's seam. The ball rests on your third finger and thumb. This grip helps you keep your wrist behind the ball. Your wrist should stay firm when you release the ball.

BOWLING ACTION

You can bowl left-handed or right-handed. The bowler shown in these pictures is right-handed. He has first paced out the number of steps he needs to take in his run up to the wicket.

1 You begin by running towards the stumps with your chest facing the front. Your run-up should be smooth with your speed building easily. Try to stay close to the stumps as you run in.

2 As you approach the stumps, push off your left foot to take a leap through the air. Your right foot should land parallel with the back crease.

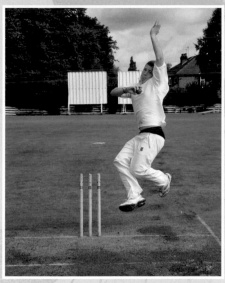

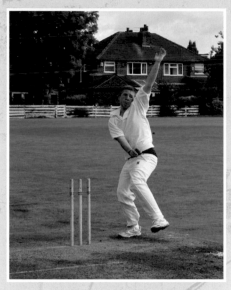

3 As you bound through the air, turn your body from facing the front to facing your side. Your left arm stretches up and out high. Your bowling arm is coiled like a spring.

4 As your bowling arm starts to uncoil and swing round, your front arm points straight down the pitch.

5 Your front foot lands with your toes pointing down the pitch. Keep your front leg firm. Your bowling arm starts to swing overarm in a large circle.

6 As your arm comes overhead, keep your wrist firm and behind the ball as you let go of it.

7 From behind, you can see how the bowler tries to keep his bowling arm high and straight and lets go of the ball at the highest point.

8 Your bowling arm keeps moving close to your body after you let go of the ball. This is called the follow-through.

TAKE A WICKET

A good bowler can control the length and the line of the ball (see page 16). Many seam bowlers aim for the ball to land on a good length around or just outside off-stump.

CONFUSE THE BATSMAN

A good length and line forces batsmen into tough decisions. Can they leave the ball or do they have to play it? This can pressure them into playing a poor shot.

Try to bowl as accurately as possible. As you improve, you may be able to surprise a batsman by bowling balls of different lengths and pace.

This bowler celebrates after bowling a slower than usual delivery to take a wicket. The batsman played his shot too early and the ball passed him to hit the stumps.

TOP TIPS

Don't try to bowl too fast at first. Try instead to aim the ball so that it lands in the same area of the pitch time and time again.

Keep your head up and regain your balance as soon as you can after bowling a ball. The batsman may hit the ball straight back to you, giving you a chance to catch it.

Don't get downhearted if a batsman hits you for fours or sixes. It happens sometimes! Keep focused on bowling accurately.

SWING AND SPIN

As your bowling skills improve, you can try different types of bowling. Swing bowling is similar to seam bowling but the ball curves in the air before landing. Spin bowling moves the ball more slowly but makes it spin in the air. This spin means that the ball may turn to the left or the right when it lands.

This is how you grip the ball for offspin bowling. A good offspin bowler lands the ball on or around off stump. The ball spins towards the leg side.

The shiny side of the ball stays to right to bowl an away swinger to a right-handed batsman. The ball curves away in the air.

TAKING A SLIP CATCH

Good bowling forces the batsman to play the ball. But the batsman does not get his foot to where the ball lands and the ball catches the edge of his bat.

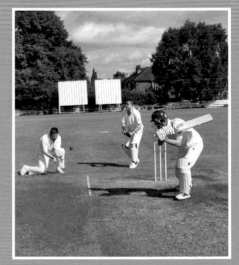

Behind the batsman, the fielding team have placed a slip fielder to the side of the wicketkeeper. The ball flies towards the slip fielder who takes a catch. The batsman is out!

FIELDING

Good fielding can win games by stopping the opposing team from scoring runs. Even if you are tired from a long spell of bowling, you must keep concentrating and field well.

GET BEHIND THE BALL

When a cricket field has an uneven, bumpy surface, this can make the ball move unpredictably. As a fielder you can help to control the path of the ball by getting your body behind it to block it. One way of doing this is called the long barrier.

THE LONG BARRIER

1 Get in line with the direction of the ball and drop down on one knee. Let that leg trail to the side to produce a long barrier.

2 Your other foot should be next to your knee with no gap between them. Gather up the ball in both hands.

3 Stand up quickly, transfer the ball into your throwing hand and take your arm back.

4 Finish your fielding with a smooth, accurate throw to a team-mate close to one of the sets of stumps.

NEAR AND FAR

Fielders are placed near the batsman and further away. Close fielders need fast reactions. They may have to make spectacular diving stops and catches. Fielders further away (known as 'in the deep') often have to chase the ball hard. They also need a strong throw to send the ball back quickly.

1 This close fielder is in a good ready position with his feet apart and his weight on the balls of his feet. His hands are ready for a quick catch.

2 Stand with your feet apart to give you a good base for throwing. Point your non-throwing arm forwards in the direction in which you want to throw the ball.

3 Throw the ball as your body weight moves from your back foot to your front foot. Your throwing arm should follow through after the ball has left your hand.

4 This fielder slides to stop the ball crossing the boundary rope for four runs. He must not let his feet or body touch the rope as he touches the ball. If he does, four runs will be added to the opposing team's score.

TOP TIPS

Keep your eye on the ball – it may change direction as it bounces.

Make sure your throw back to the stumps is as accurate as possible.

If you are the bowler or wicketkeeper, get close to the stumps and be ready for a throw from a team-mate.

CATCH IT!

Catches are an important way in which fielders can get the opposing team's batsmen out. You will also need to catch the ball cleanly when a team-mate throws it to you.

DON'T BE SCARED!

Some players are a little scared of a speeding cricket ball at first, but catching doesn't hurt, if you do it right! Make sure you watch the ball right into your hands. Aim for the ball to land where your fingers join your palm rather than on the ends of your fingers.

HIGH CATCHES

1 This fielder has to catch a ball that's coming from high in the air. She runs hard to get into position.

2 She moves her arms up, keeping her eye on the ball. Her fingers are spread a little to make a large cup for the ball to land in.

3 As the ball arrives the fielder clasps her fingers around the ball. She will bring it down and towards her chest to keep it safe.

 TOP TIPS Practise catching as often as you can. You can throw and catch with a friend, throwing the ball from different distances and heights.

You can also practise on your own, bouncing a softer ball such as a tennis ball off a wall.

1 Sometimes you can take a low catch when you are fielding close to a batsman. You need a good wide stance with your knees bent and your hands out in front of you.

2 Try to catch with both hands and allow your fingers to close around the ball. Watch the ball right into your hands.

3 Cushion the ball's landing by taking your hands back as you catch it. This will help stop the ball from bouncing out of your grasp.

PRO PLAY

Sometimes, the ball will fly to your side and you will have to make a one-handed catch, as Jimmy Anderson of England does here. Keep your eye on the ball, stretch to reach it and try to get your other hand on the ball as quickly as possible.

KEEPING WICKET

Wicketkeepers are the goalkeepers of cricket. Once a ball has been bowled and passes a batsman, wicketkeepers try to stop the ball to prevent runs being scored. If the batsman touches the ball with his bat, they may catch the ball and get him out.

QUICK REACTIONS

A wicketkeeper has to stay alert for every ball, whether it comes straight towards the stumps, to the offside of the stumps or wide down either side of them. Wicketkeepers have to wear protective clothing, including large leg pads and padded gloves.

1 This wicketkeeper is ready for action, crouching behind the stumps with his knees bent and his head up.

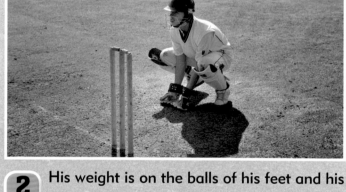

2 His weight is on the balls of his feet and his hands are close together. His eyes watch the ball as it leaves the bowler's hand.

3 As the ball comes towards him, the keeper starts to rise from his crouched position. He takes a small step to his right so that he is in line with the ball.

4 His gloves stay together as the ball arrives, forming a large cup for the ball to land in.

5 He bends his elbows and takes his arms back as the ball lands in his gloves. This action helps stop the ball bouncing out of his gloves.

If the batsman hits the ball and runs, the wicketkeeper runs up to the stumps. He is now ready to receive the ball thrown-in by his team-mate.

Sometimes, he may gather the ball and use it to hit the stumps to run out an opponent.

PRO PLAY

England wicketkeeper Sarah Taylor reacts quickly, gathering the ball and stumping India's Rumeli Dhar. Knocking the bails off with the ball before a batter is back in their crease will mean that the batter is out, stumped.

As wicketkeeper you must decide how far to stand from the stumps. If your team-mate bowls fast, stand further back.

MAKING THE TEAM

Talent will only take you so far. To become a good cricketer, you have to work hard at improving your bowling, batting and fielding skills.

PRACTISE AND IMPROVE

The best way to improve your skills is through a lot of practice. Team training sessions are very useful because your coach can point out little improvements in technique that will make a big difference. But you can also practise skills such as catching and fielding away from the team with just one or two friends.

IN TRAINING

1 Stretching your muscles before training or playing is really important. These Kwik cricketers are all performing side stretches.

2 Batsman and bowlers can practise their skills in cricket nets.

3 This coach is helping one cricketer with his long barrier fielding position. Listen to your coach's advice and you will improve quickly.

These three cricketers are practising their catching and handling skills. They throw two balls between the three of them. They try to keep the throws and catches as smooth and quick as possible.

PRO PLAY

Top players such as Sri Lanka's Muttiah Muralitharan practise their basic skills almost every day. This helps make them top international players. Muralitharan has taken more wickets than anyone else in Test cricket and in One Day Internationals.

TOP TIPS

Cricket is a game you play with your brain as well as your body. Concentrate hard whenever you practise or play.

If you make a mistake in a game, try to stay positive. Put it out of your mind and focus on the rest of the match.

Support your team-mates. Encourage them and don't criticise if they get out, bowl badly or drop a catch.

GLOSSARY

appeal
When the fielding team think they may have got a batsman out and ask the umpire, "howzat!" (how is that?).

bails
The small cylinders of wood placed on top of the cricket stumps to form a wicket.

boundary
The edge of the cricket ground, usually marked by a rope.

bowled
One way that a batsman can be out. It occurs when the bowler bowls the ball which hits the stumps and knocks off one or both bails.

catches
When fielders gather the ball in their hands after it has hit the batsman's glove or bat and before the ball touches the ground. A successful catch means the batsman is out.

cover drive
A type of cricket shot hit forward through the cover area of the pitch with a straight bat.

creases
Line markings around parts of a cricket pitch.

grip
How you hold the handle of a bat.

innings
The period when batsmen bat until they are out. It can also mean the entire team's turn to bat.

Kwik cricket
A simpler form of cricket for young players with everyone getting a turn to bowl and bat.

LBW
Short for leg before wicket, it is a way in which batsmen can be out by the ball hitting their leg pads when they are standing in front of their stumps.

leg glance
A delicate shot in which the batsman angles the ball so it runs away down the leg side behind the batsman.

line and length
Words that describe the direction the ball travels after it leaves the bowler's hand (the line) and how far up the pitch it lands on its first bounce (the length).

long barrier
A method of fielding a ball that is running along the ground by using your leg and body as a second barrier behind your hands.

nets
A training and practice area at many cricket grounds made up of corridors of pitches divided by nets to stop the ball travelling far.

overs
A series of six correct deliveries bowled by a bowler from one end of the pitch.

pads
Protective padded shields worn around the lower leg by batsmen and wicketkeepers.

slip fielder
A fielder who stands to the side of the wicketkeeper and looks to catch the ball if it clips the edge of the bat.

stumps
The wooden poles that stand upright at each end of the pitch and which, with the bails, form a wicket.

sweep shot
A type of shot in which the ball is swept around behind the batsman with the batsman's back knee very low to the ground.

umpires The officials who run a cricket match and make sure the players follow all the laws of cricket.

wicketkeeper Member of a cricket team who stands behind the stumps and fields the ball should it pass the batsman.

wides Deliveries where the ball bounces too high or wide of the stumps for the batsman to reach it easily.

RESOURCES

BOOKS

Sporting Skills: Cricket –
Clive Gifford,
Wayland, 2008
For slightly older readers, this
book goes into the techniques
and tactics of cricket.

Starting Sport Cricket –
Rebecca Hunter, Watts, 2006
A simple guide to learning to play
the sport.

Training To Succeed: Cricket –
Edward Way, Watts, 2009
This book looks at the lives of
a group of teenage cricketers
who are hoping to make it in
professional cricket.

WEBSITES

http://news.bbc.co.uk/sport1/hi/
cricket/skills/default.stm
The BBC's excellent cricket
webpages include videos of
cricketing skills and a Get Involved
section listing people to contact
for junior cricket.

http://www.ecb.co.uk/
development/kids/
This website tells you all about the
different forms of cricket you can
play. It also has stats listings and
videos to watch.

http://www.cricket4kids.com/
This website has plenty of
information about how to get
started playing cricket.

There's a lot to learn when you
start out playing cricket. Most
important of all is to remember
to have fun! Cricket is great fun
to learn as part of a team. If you
have not played before, why not
round up some friends so that
together you can all...Get Sporty!

appeal 11

backlift 13
backwards defensive 13, 14
backwards forcing shot 14
bails 6, 11
ball 4, 5, 7, 8, 10, 11, 12, 13, 14, 15, 16, 17, 18, 19, 20, 21, 22, 23, 26, 27
bat 4, 5, 7, 8, 13, 15
batting 4, 5, 7, 8, 9, 10, 11, 12, 13, 14, 15, 16, 17, 18, 20, 21, 23, 28
boundary 10, 17, 23
bowling 4, 7, 8, 9, 10, 11, 13, 14, 17, 18, 19, 20, 21, 23, 26, 28

catches 6, 21, 23, 24, 25, 26, 28
clothing 7, 8, 26
coach 10, 13, 14, 18, 28
cover drive 15
creases 6, 10, 11, 12, 18
cut shot 17

fielding 4, 5, 9, 14, 22, 23, 24, 25, 28
forward defensive 13, 14, 17

grip 7, 12, 18

helmet 7

innings 4, 9, 17

Kwik cricket 8, 9, 11, 28

laws 10
leg glance 15
line and length 16, 20
long barrier 22

nets 14, 28
no ball 10

out 5, 9, 11, 14, 21, 24, 26, 27
    bowled 9
    caught 11, 14, 21, 26
    handled ball 11
    lbw 11
    run out 5, 27
overs 4, 8, 9

pads 7, 11, 13, 26
pitch 4, 5, 6, 8, 17, 18, 19
placing fielders 20, 23
push shot 14

runs 4, 5, 9, 10, 14, 16, 17, 23

scoring 4, 9, 10, 14, 16, 23
slip fielder 21
stance 12, 25
stumps 5, 6, 8, 11, 13, 15, 17, 18, 20, 22, 23, 26, 27
sweep shot 16

taking guard 17
throws 22, 23

umpires 10, 11, 17

wicket 4, 6, 18
wicketkeeper 4, 7, 9, 21, 23, 26, 27
wides 10